Duke Ellington

Arrangements by Chip Henderson, Bill LaFleur, and Masa Takahashi

ISBN 978-1-4234-3700-0

HAL•LEONARD® CORPORATION

7777 W. BLUEMOUND RD. P.O. BOX 13819 MILWAUKEE, WI 53213

Visit Hal Leonard Online at **www.halleonard.com**

C-Jam Blues

By Duke Ellington

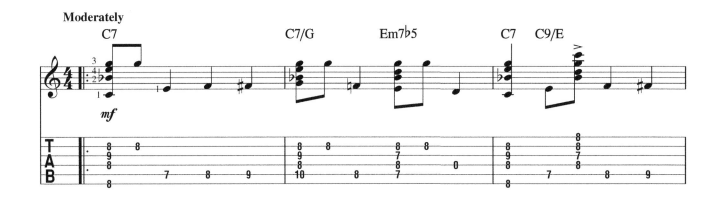

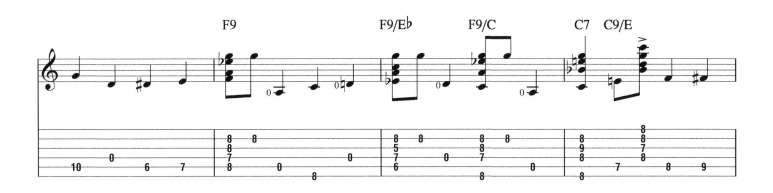

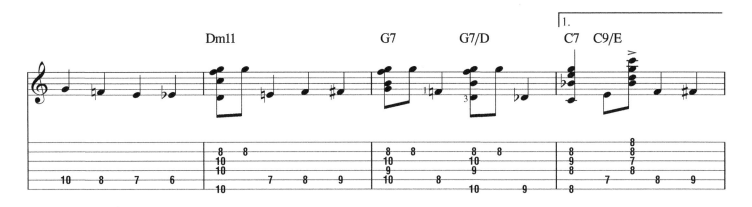

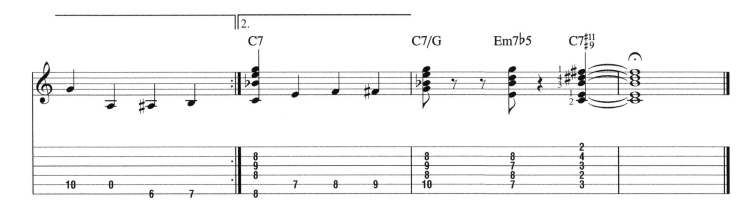

Come Sunday

from BLACK, BROWN & BEIGE
By Duke Ellington

Caravan

Words and Music by Duke Ellington, Irving Mills and Juan Tizol

Cotton Tail

By Duke Ellington

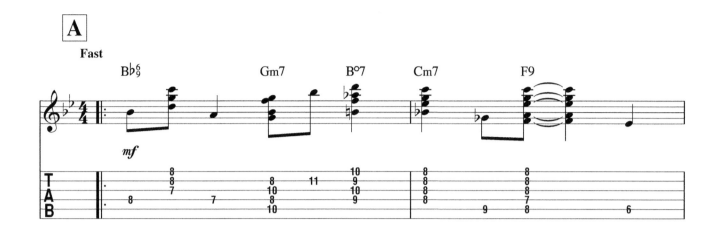

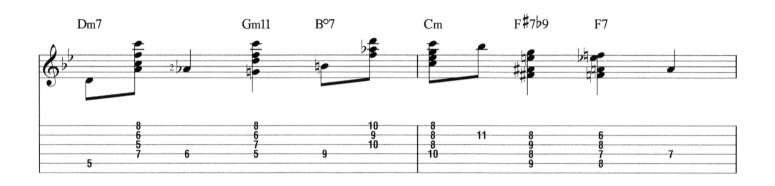

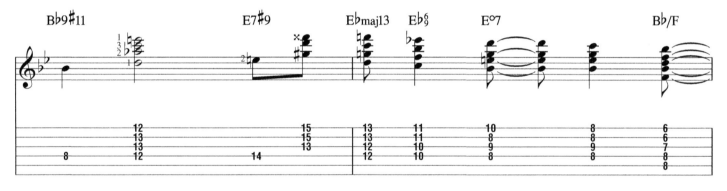

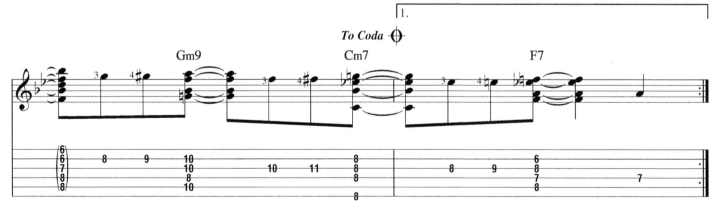

Do Nothin' till You Hear from Me

Words and Music by Duke Ellington and Bob Russell

Don't Get Around Much Anymore

Words and Music by Duke Ellington and Bob Russell

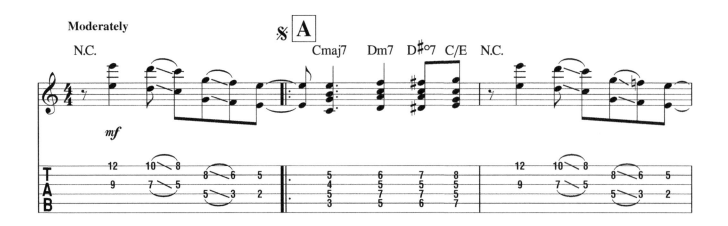

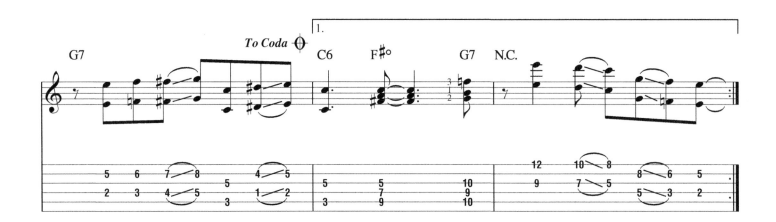

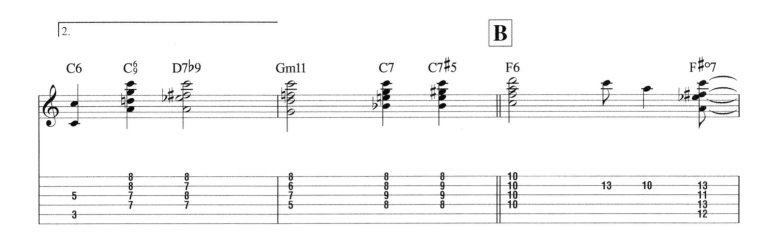

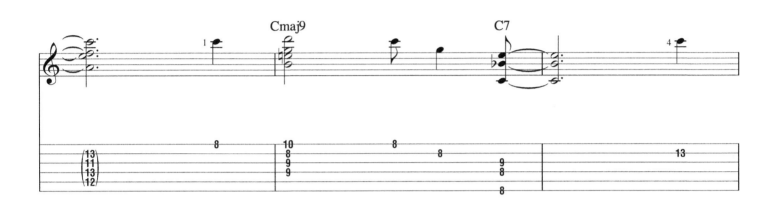

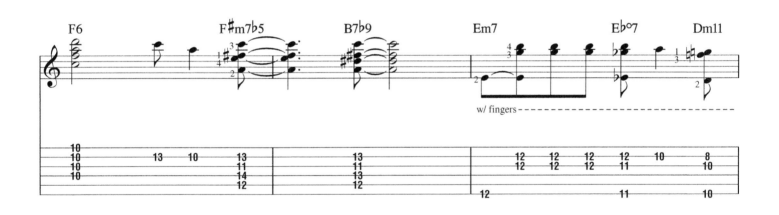

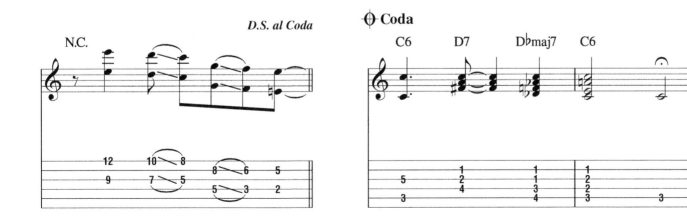

I Didn't Know About You

Words by Bob Russell
Music by Duke Ellington

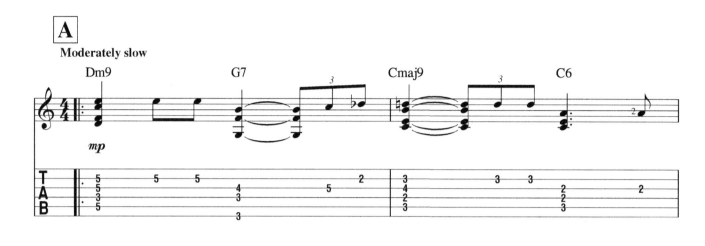

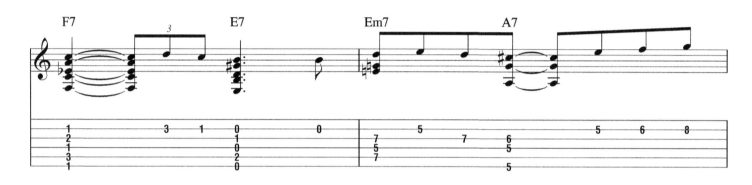

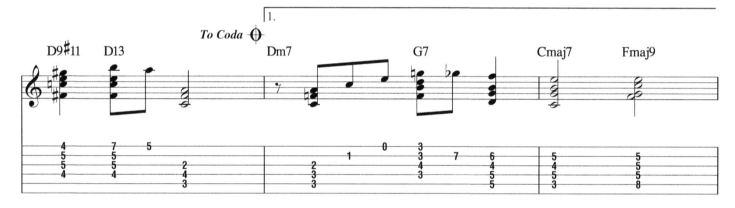

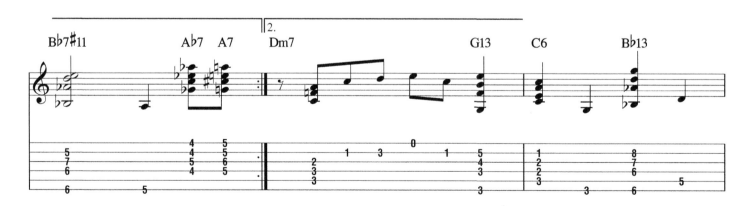

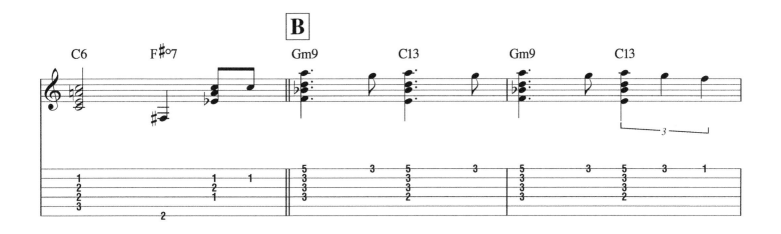

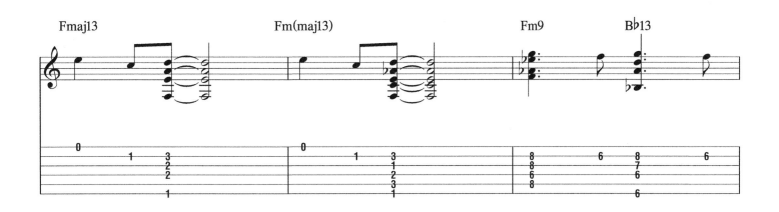

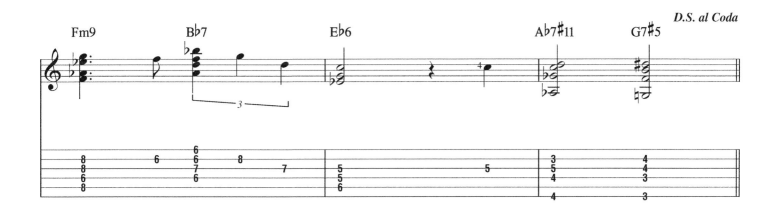

I Got It Bad and That Ain't Good

Words by Paul Francis Webster
Music by Duke Ellington

In a Sentimental Mood

By Duke Ellington

I Let a Song Go Out of My Heart

Words and Music by Duke Ellington, Henry Nemo, John Redmond and Irving Mills

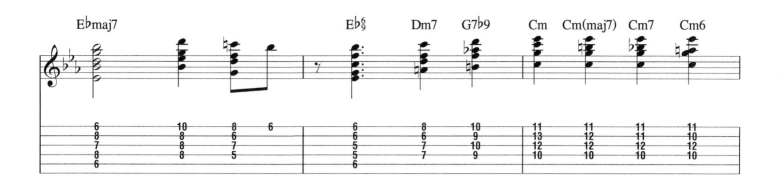

D.C. al Coda

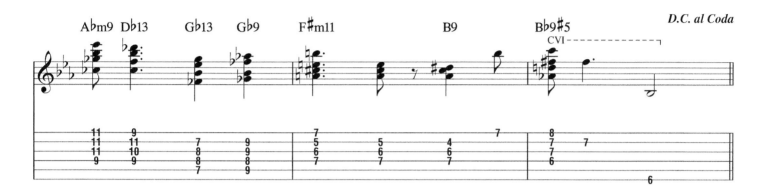

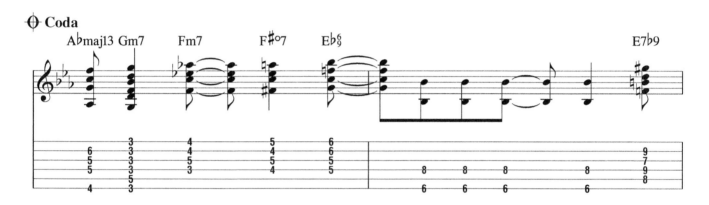

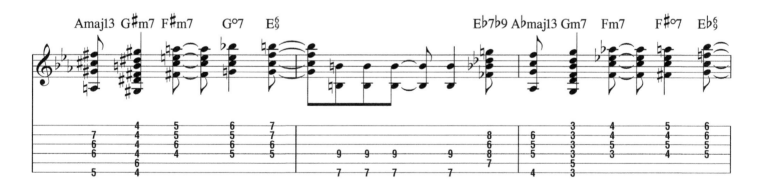

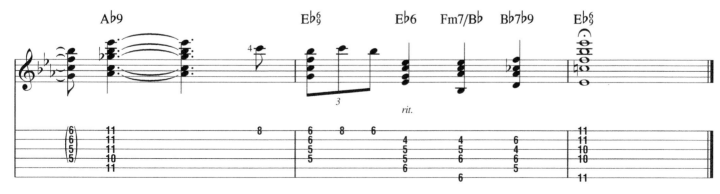

I'm Beginning to See the Light

Words and Music by Don George, Johnny Hodges, Duke Ellington and Harry James

I'm Just a Lucky So and So

Words by Mack David
Music by Duke Ellington

In a Mellow Tone

By Duke Ellington

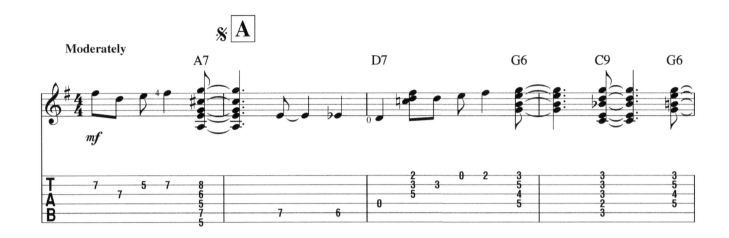

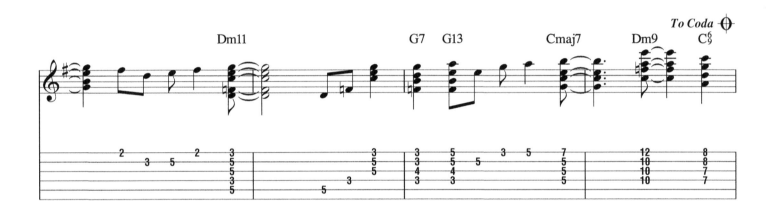

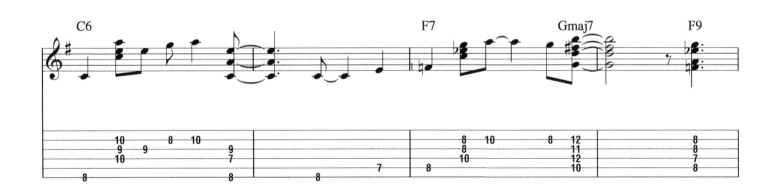

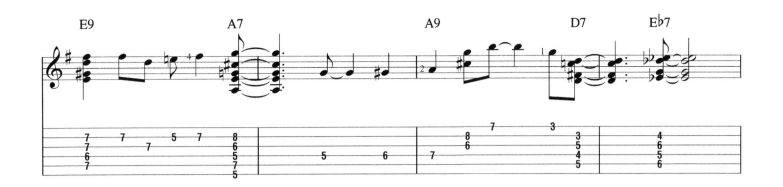

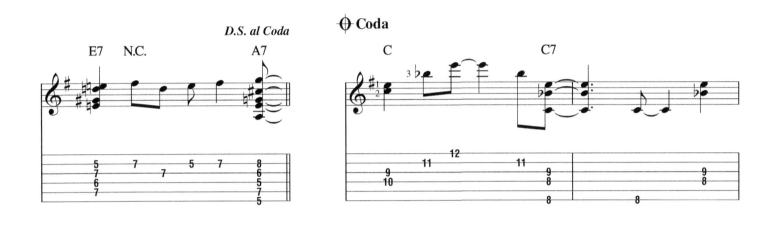

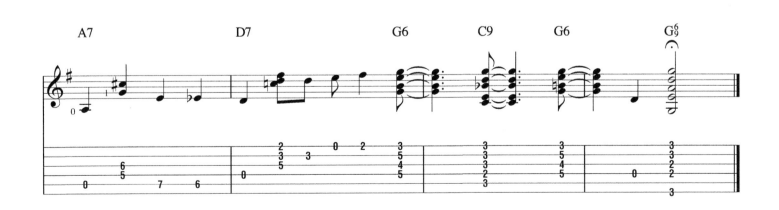

Isfahan

from FAR EAST SUITE
By Duke Ellington and Billy Strayhorn

A

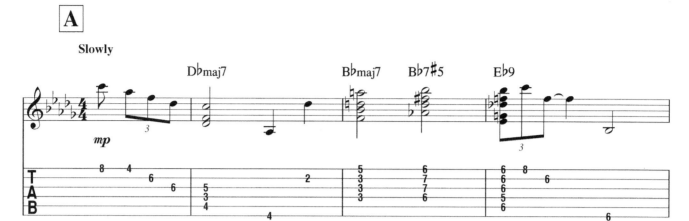

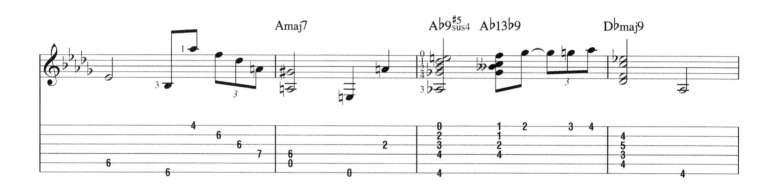

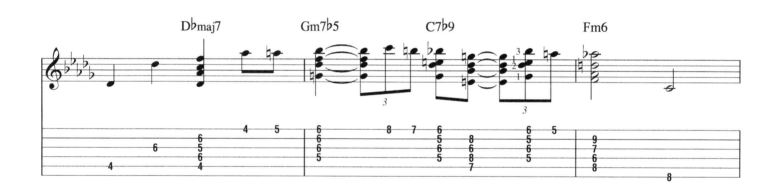

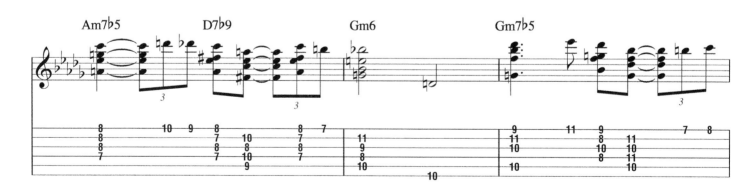

It Don't Mean a Thing
(If It Ain't Got That Swing)

Words and Music by Duke Ellington and Irving Mills

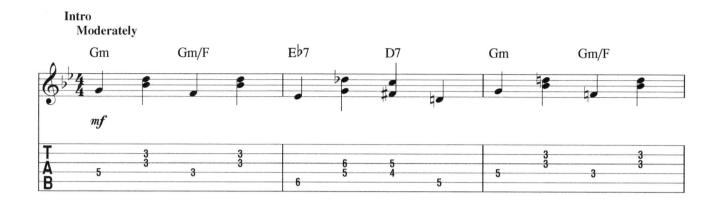

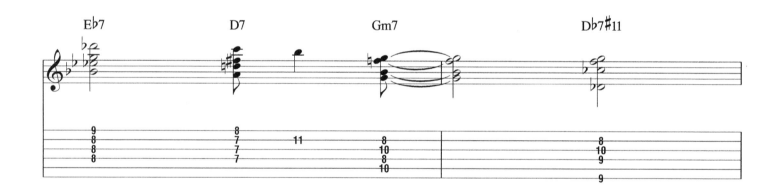

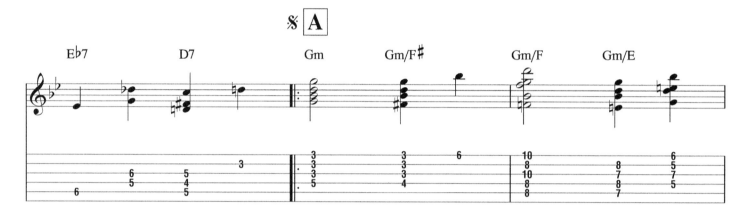

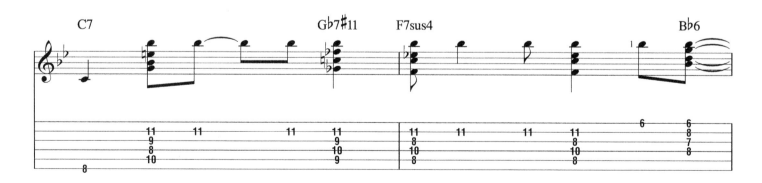

Just Squeeze Me

(But Don't Tease Me)

Words by Lee Gaines
Music by Duke Ellington

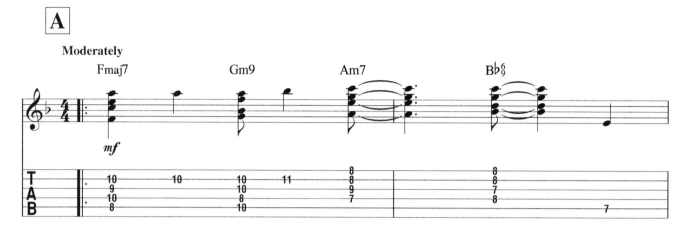

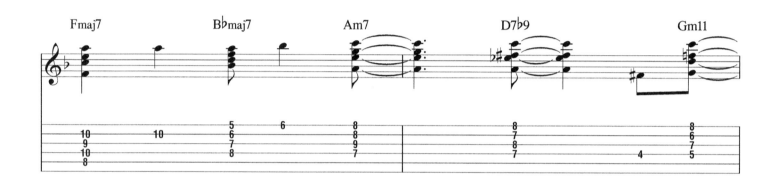

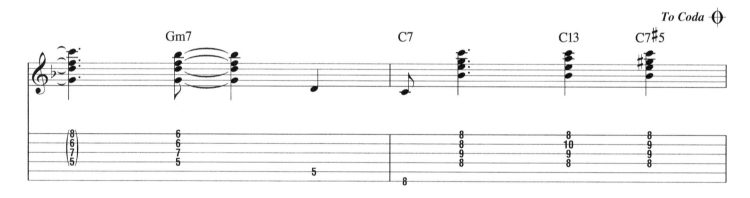

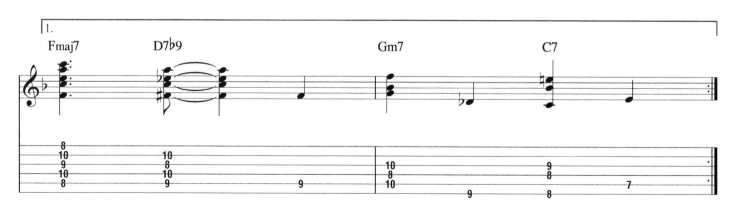

Love You Madly

By Duke Ellington

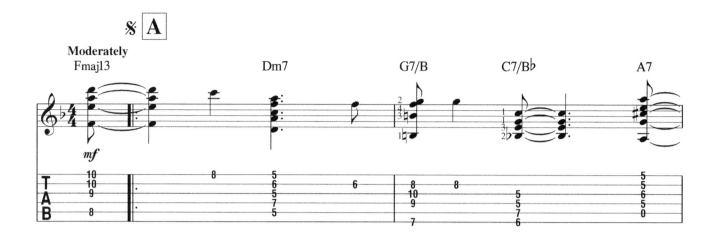

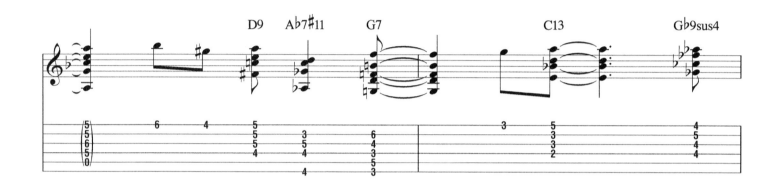

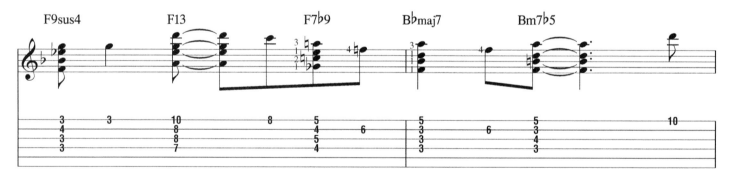

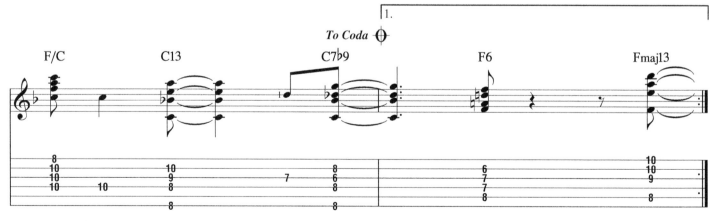

Mood Indigo

Words and Music by Duke Ellington, Irving Mills and Albany Bigard

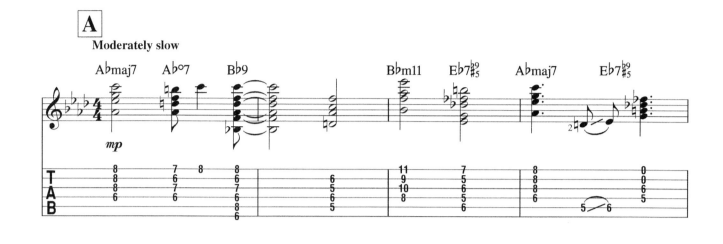

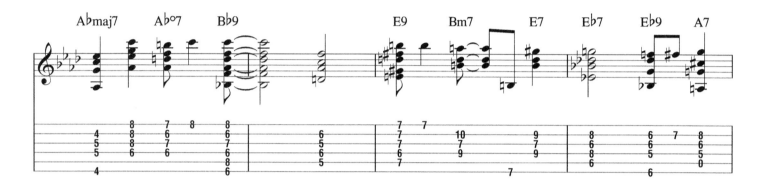

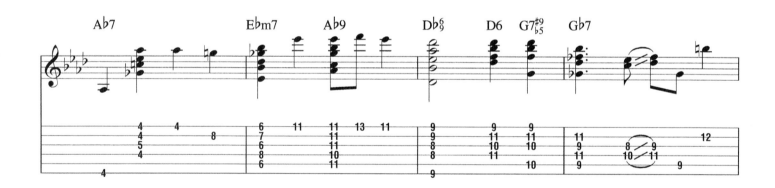

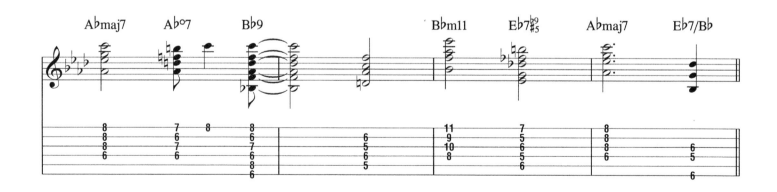

Perdido

Words by Harry Lenk and Ervin Drake
Music by Juan Tizol

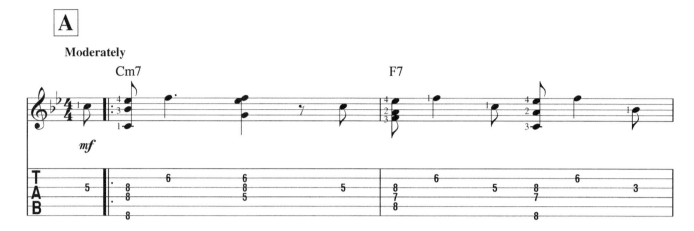

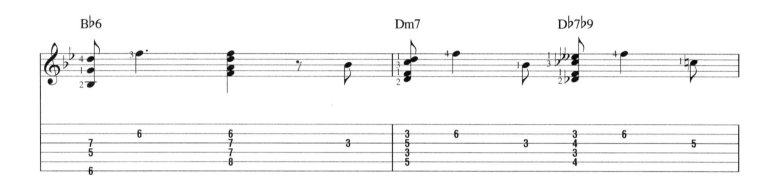

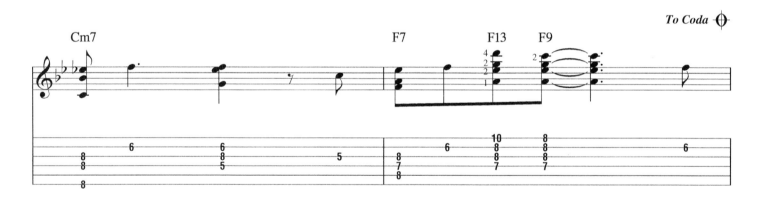

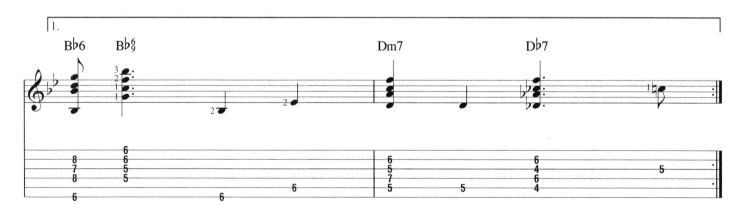

Prelude to a Kiss

Words by Irving Gordon and Irving Mills
Music by Duke Ellington

Sophisticated Lady

Words and Music by Duke Ellington, Irving Mills and Mitchell Parish

Satin Doll

By Duke Ellington

Solitude

Words and Music by Duke Ellington, Eddie De Lange and Irving Mills

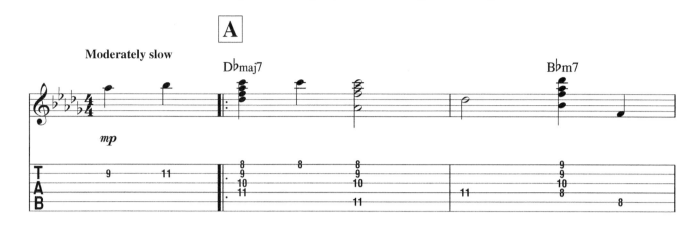

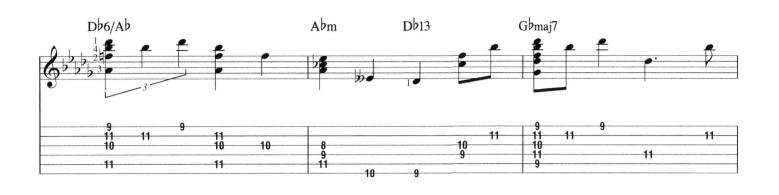

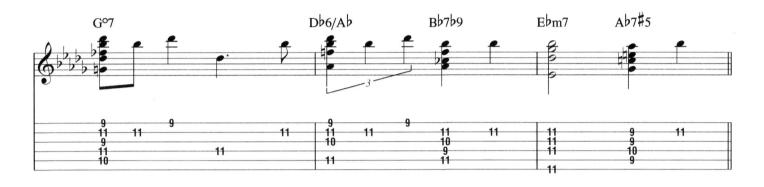

C

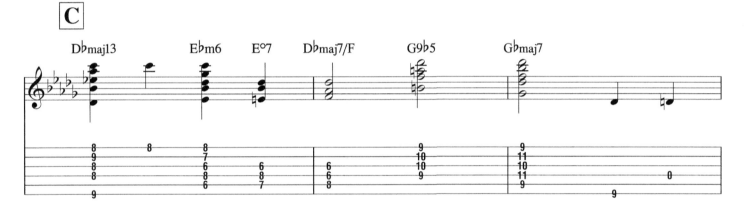

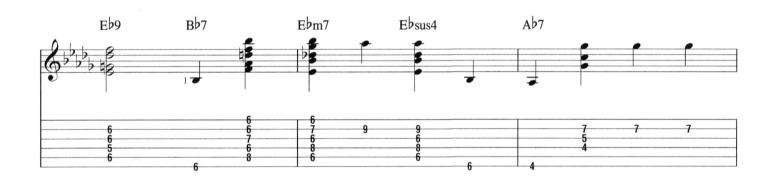

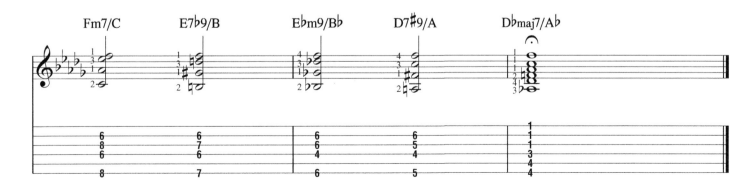

Things Ain't What They Used to Be

By Mercer Ellington

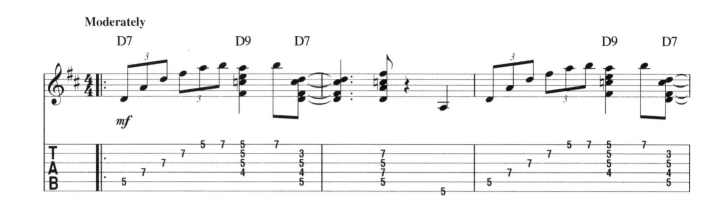

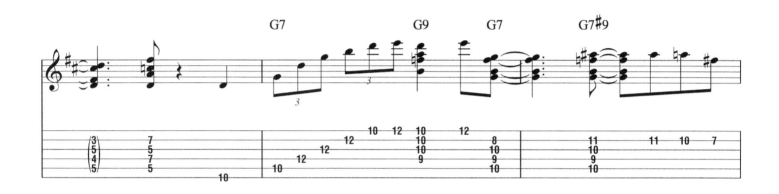

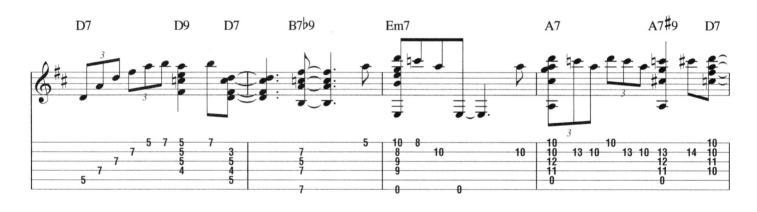

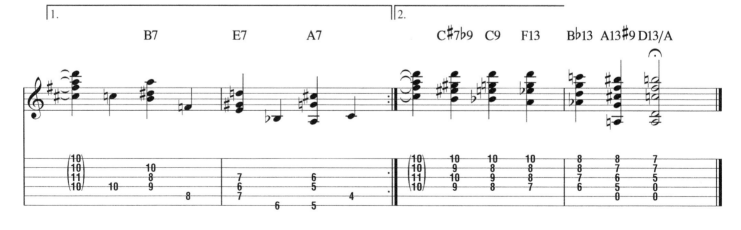

Warm Valley

By Duke Ellington

PLAY THE CLASSICS

JAZZ FOLIOS FOR GUITARISTS

BEST OF JAZZ GUITAR

by Wolf Marshall • Signature Licks

In this book/audio pack, Wolf Marshall provides a hands-on analysis of 10 of the most frequently played tunes in the jazz genre, as played by the leading guitarists of all time. Features: All the Things You Are • How Insensitive • I'll Remember April • So What • Yesterdays • and more.
00695586 Book/Online Audio................................$29.99

GUITAR STANDARDS

Classic Jazz Masters Series

16 classic jazz guitar performances transcribed note for note with tablature: All of You (Kenny Burrell) • Easter Parade (Herb Ellis) • I'll Remember April (Grant Green) • Lover Man (Django Reinhardt) • Song for My Father (George Benson) • The Way You Look Tonight (Wes Montgomery) • and more. Includes a discography.
00699143 Guitar Transcriptions $14.95

JAZZ CLASSICS FOR SOLO GUITAR

arranged by Robert B. Yelin

This collection includes excellent chord melody arrangements in standard notation and tablature for 35 all-time jazz favorites: April in Paris • Cry Me a River • Day by Day • God Bless' the Child • It Might as Well Be Spring • Lover • My Romance • Nuages • Satin Doll • Tenderly • Unchained Melody • Wave • and more!
00699279 Solo Guitar $19.99

JAZZ FAVORITES FOR SOLO GUITAR

arranged by Robert B. Yelin

This fantastic 35-song collection includes lush chord melody arrangements in standard notation and tab: Autumn in New York • Call Me Irresponsible • How Deep Is the Ocean • I Could Write a Book • The Lady Is a Tramp • Mood Indigo • Polka Dots and Moonbeams • Solitude • Take the "A" Train • Where or When • more.
00699278 Solo Guitar $19.99

JAZZ GEMS FOR SOLO GUITAR

arranged by Robert B. Yelin

35 great solo arrangements of jazz classics, including: After You've Gone • Alice in Wonderland • The Christmas Song • Four • Meditation • Stompin' at the Savoy • Sweet and Lovely • Waltz for Debby • Yardbird Suite • You'll Never Walk Alone • You've Changed • and more.
00699617 Solo Guitar $19.99

JAZZ GUITAR BIBLE

The one book that has all of the jazz guitar classics transcribed note-for-note, with standard notation and tablature. Includes over 30 songs: Body and Soul • Girl Talk • I'll Remember April • In a Sentimental Mood • My Funny Valentine • Nuages • Satin Doll • So What • Stardust • Take Five • Tangerine • Yardbird Suite • and more.
00690466 Guitar Recorded Versions $24.99

JAZZ GUITAR CHORD MELODIES

arranged & performed by Dan Towey

This book/CD pack includes complete solo performances of 12 standards, including: All the Things You Are • Body and Soul • My Romance • How Insensitive • My One and Only Love • and more. The arrangements are performance level and range in difficulty from intermediate to advanced.
00698988 Book/CD Pack..$19.95

JAZZ GUITAR PLAY-ALONG

Guitar Play-Along Volume 16

With this book/audio pack, all you have to do is follow the tab, listen to the online audio to hear how the guitar should sound, and then play along using the separate backing tracks. 8 songs: All Blues • Bluesette • Footprints • How Insensitive (Insensatez) • Misty • Satin Doll • Stella by Starlight • Tenor Madness.
00699584 Book/Online Audio................................$16.99

JAZZ STANDARDS FOR FINGERSTYLE GUITAR

20 songs, including: All the Things You Are • Autumn Leaves • Bluesette • Body and Soul • Fly Me to the Moon • The Girl from Ipanema • How Insensitive • I've Grown Accustomed to Her Face • My Funny Valentine • Satin Doll • Stompin' at the Savoy • and more.
00699029 Fingerstyle Guitar $17.99

JAZZ STANDARDS FOR SOLO GUITAR

arranged by Robert B. Yelin

35 chord melody guitar arrangements, including: Ain't Misbehavin' • Autumn Leaves • Bewitched • Cherokee • Darn That Dream • Girl Talk • I've Got You Under My Skin • Lullaby of Birdland • My Funny Valentine • A Nightingale Sang in Berkeley Square • Stella by Starlight • The Very Thought of You • and more.
00699277 Solo Guitar $19.99

101 MUST-KNOW JAZZ LICKS

by Wolf Marshall

Add a jazz feel and flavor to your playing! 101 definitive licks, plus demonstration audio, from every major jazz guitar style, neatly organized into easy-to-use categories. They're all here: swing and pre-bop, bebop, post-bop modern jazz, hard bop and cool jazz, modal jazz, soul jazz and postmodern jazz.
00695433 Book/Online Audio................................$19.99

HAL•LEONARD®

Visit Hal Leonard Online at **www.halleonard.com**

Prices, contents and availability subject to change without notice.

0322
135

IMPROVE YOUR IMPROV
AND OTHER JAZZ TECHNIQUES WITH BOOKS FROM HAL LEONARD

JAZZ GUITAR
HAL LEONARD GUITAR METHOD
by Jeff Schroedl

The Hal Leonard Jazz Guitar Method is your complete guide to learning jazz guitar. This book uses real jazz songs to teach the basics of accompanying and improvising jazz guitar in the style of Wes Montgomery, Joe Pass, Tal Farlow, Charlie Christian, Pat Martino, Barney Kessel, Jim Hall, and many others.
00695359 Book/Online Audio $22.99

AMAZING PHRASING
50 WAYS TO IMPROVE YOUR
IMPROVISATIONAL SKILLS • *by Tom Kolb*

This book explores all the main components necessary for crafting well-balanced rhythmic and melodic phrases. It also explains how these phrases are put together to form cohesive solos. Many styles are covered – rock, blues, jazz, fusion, country, Latin, funk and more – and all of the concepts are backed up with musical examples.
00695583 Book/Online Audio $22.99

BEST OF JAZZ GUITAR
by Wolf Marshall • Signature Licks

In this book/audio pack, Wolf Marshall provides a hands-on analysis of 10 of the most frequently played tunes in the jazz genre, as played by the leading guitarists of all time. Each selection includes technical analysis and performance notes, biographical sketches, and authentic matching audio with backing tracks.
00695586 Book/Online Audio $29.99

CHORD-MELODY PHRASES FOR GUITAR
by Ron Eschete • REH ProLessons Series

Expand your chord-melody chops with these outstanding jazz phrases! This book covers: chord substitutions, chromatic movements, contrary motion, pedal tones, inner-voice movements, reharmonization techniques, and much more. Includes standard notation and tab, and online audio.
00695628 Book/Online Audio $17.99

CHORDS FOR JAZZ GUITAR
THE COMPLETE GUIDE TO COMPING,
CHORD MELODY AND CHORD SOLOING • *by Charlton Johnson*

This book/audio pack will teach you how to play jazz chords all over the fretboard in a variety of styles and progressions. It covers: voicings, progressions, jazz chord theory, comping, chord melody, chord soloing, voice leading and many more topics. The audio offers 98 full-band demo tracks. No tablature.
00695706 Book/Online Audio $19.99

FRETBOARD ROADMAPS – JAZZ GUITAR
THE ESSENTIAL GUITAR PATTERNS
THAT ALL THE PROS KNOW AND USE • *by Fred Sokolow*

This book will get guitarists playing lead & rhythm anywhere on the fretboard, in any key! It teaches a variety of lead guitar styles using moveable patterns, double-note licks, sliding pentatonics and more, through easy-to-follow diagrams and instructions. The online audio includes 54 full-demo tracks.
00695354 Book/Online Audio $17.99

JAZZ IMPROVISATION FOR GUITAR
by Les Wise • REH ProLessons Series

This book/audio will allow you to make the transition from playing disjointed scales and arpeggios to playing melodic jazz solos that maintain continuity and interest for the listener. Topics covered include: tension and resolution, major scale, melodic minor scale, and harmonic minor scale patterns, common licks and substitution techniques, creating altered tension, and more! Features standard notation and tab, and online audio.
00695657 Book/Online Audio $19.99

JAZZ RHYTHM GUITAR
THE COMPLETE GUIDE
by Jack Grassel

This book/audio pack will help rhythm guitarists better understand: chord symbols and voicings, comping styles and patterns, equipment, accessories and set-up, the fingerboard, chord theory, and much more. The accompanying online audio includes 74 full-band tracks.
00695654 Book/Online Audio $24.99

JAZZ SOLOS FOR GUITAR
LEAD GUITAR IN THE STYLES OF TAL FARLOW,
BARNEY KESSEL, WES MONTGOMERY, JOE PASS, JOHNNY SMITH
by Les Wise

Examine the solo concepts of the masters with this book including phrase-by-phrase performance notes, tips on arpeggio substitution, scale substitution, tension and resolution, jazz-blues, chord soloing, and more. The audio includes full demonstration and rhythm-only tracks.
00695447 Book/Online Audio $19.99

100 JAZZ LESSONS
Guitar Lesson Goldmine Series
by John Heussenstamm and Paul Silbergleit

Featuring 100 individual modules covering a giant array of topics, each lesson includes detailed instruction with playing examples presented in standard notation and tablature. You'll also get extremely useful tips, scale diagrams, and more to reinforce your learning experience, plus audio featuring performance demos of all the examples in the book!
00696454 Book/Online Audio $24.99

101 MUST-KNOW JAZZ LICKS
A QUICK, EASY REFERENCE GUIDE
FOR ALL GUITARISTS • *by Wolf Marshall*

Here are 101 definitive licks, plus demonstration audio, from every major jazz guitar style, neatly organized into easy-to-use categories. They're all here: swing and pre-bop, bebop, post-bop modern jazz, hard bop and cool jazz, modal jazz, soul jazz and postmodern jazz. Includes an introduction, tips, and a list of suggested recordings.
00695433 Book/Online Audio $19.99

SWING AND BIG BAND GUITAR
FOUR-TO-THE-BAR COMPING IN THE STYLE OF
FREDDIE GREEN • *by Charlton Johnson*

This unique package teaches the essentials of swing and big band styles, including chord voicings, inversions, substitutions; time and groove, reading charts, chord reduction, and expansion; sample songs, patterns, progressions, and exercises; chord reference library; and online audio with over 50 full-demo examples. Uses chord grids – no tablature.
00695147 Book/Online Audio $22.99

Get Better at Guitar

...with these Great Guitar Instruction Books from Hal Leonard!

101 GUITAR TIPS
STUFF ALL THE PROS KNOW AND USE
by Adam St. James
This book contains invaluable guidance on everything from scales and music theory to truss rod adjustments, proper recording studio set-ups, and much more.
00695737 Book/Online Audio $17.99

AMAZING PHRASING
by Tom Kolb
This book/audio pack explores all the main components necessary for crafting well-balanced rhythmic and melodic phrases. It also explains how these phrases are put together to form cohesive solos. The companion audio contains 89 demo tracks, most with full-band backing.
00695583 Book/Online Audio $22.99

ARPEGGIOS FOR THE MODERN GUITARIST
by Tom Kolb
Using this no-nonsense book with online audio, guitarists will learn to apply and execute all types of arpeggio forms using a variety of techniques, including alternate picking, sweep picking, tapping, string skipping, and legato.
00695862 Book/Online Audio $22.99

BLUES YOU CAN USE
by John Ganapes
This comprehensive source for learning blues guitar is designed to develop both your lead and rhythm playing. Includes: 21 complete solos • blues chords, progressions and riffs • turnarounds • movable scales and soloing techniques • string bending • utilizing the entire fingerboard • and more.
00142420 Book/Online Media..................................$22.99

CONNECTING PENTATONIC PATTERNS
by Tom Kolb
If you've been finding yourself trapped in the pentatonic box, this book is for you! This hands-on book with online audio offers examples for guitar players of all levels, from beginner to advanced. Study this book faithfully, and soon you'll be soloing all over the neck with the greatest of ease.
00696445 Book/Online Audio $24.99

FRETBOARD MASTERY
by Troy Stetina
Untangle the mysterious regions of the guitar fretboard and unlock your potential. This book familiarizes you with all the shapes you need to know by applying them in real musical examples, thereby reinforcing and reaffirming your newfound knowledge.
00695331 Book/Online Audio $22.99

GUITAR AEROBICS
by Troy Nelson
Here is a daily dose of guitar "vitamins" to keep your chops fine tuned! Musical styles include rock, blues, jazz, metal, country, and funk. Techniques taught include alternate picking, arpeggios, sweep picking, string skipping, legato, string bending, and rhythm guitar.
00695946 Book/Online Audio $24.99

GUITAR CLUES
OPERATION PENTATONIC
by Greg Koch
Whether you're new to improvising or have been doing it for a while, this book/audio pack will provide loads of delicious licks and tricks that you can use right away, from volume swells and chicken pickin' to intervallic and chordal ideas.
00695827 Book/Online Audio $19.99

PAT METHENY – GUITAR ETUDES
Over the years, in many master classes and workshops around the world, Pat has demonstrated the kind of daily workout he puts himself through. This book includes a collection of 14 guitar etudes he created to help you limber up, improve picking technique and build finger independence.
00696587..$17.99

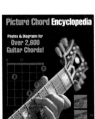

PICTURE CHORD ENCYCLOPEDIA
This comprehensive guitar chord resource for all playing styles and levels features five voicings of 44 chord qualities for all twelve keys – 2,640 chords in all! For each, there is a clearly illustrated chord frame, as well as *an actual photo* of the chord being played!.
00695224..$22.99

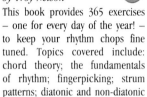

RHYTHM GUITAR 365
by Troy Nelson
This book provides 365 exercises – one for every day of the year! – to keep your rhythm chops fine tuned. Topics covered include: chord theory; the fundamentals of rhythm; fingerpicking; strum patterns; diatonic and non-diatonic progressions; triads; major and minor keys; and more.
00103627 Book/Online Audio $27.99

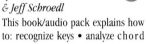

SCALE CHORD RELATIONSHIPS
by Michael Mueller & Jeff Schroedl
This book/audio pack explains how to: recognize keys • analyze chord progressions • use the modes • play over nondiatonic harmony • use harmonic and melodic minor scales • use symmetrical scales • incorporate exotic scales • and much more!
00695563 Book/Online Audio $17.99

SPEED MECHANICS FOR LEAD GUITAR
by Troy Stetina
Take your playing to the stratosphere with this advanced lead book which will help you develop speed and precision in today's explosive playing styles. Learn the fastest ways to achieve speed and control, secrets to make your practice time really count, and how to open your ears and make your musical ideas more solid and tangible.
00699323 Book/Online Audio $22.99

TOTAL ROCK GUITAR
by Troy Stetina
This comprehensive source for learning rock guitar is designed to develop both lead and rhythm playing. It covers: getting a tone that rocks • open chords, power chords and barre chords • riffs, scales and licks • string bending, strumming, and harmonics • and more.
00695246 Book/Online Audio $22.99

Guitar World Presents
STEVE VAI'S GUITAR WORKOUT
In this book, Steve Vai reveals his path to virtuoso enlightenment with two challenging guitar workouts – one 10-hour and one 30-hour – which include scale and chord exercises, ear training, sight-reading, music theory, and much more.
00119643..$16.99

Prices, contents, and availability subject to change without notice.